REVERSING SATANIC JUDGEMENTS IN HEAVENLY COURTS

Prayers for Cleansing Ancestral Bloodlines in the Courts of Heaven

PRAYER M. MADUEKE

PRAYER PUBLICATIONS
UNITED STATES

Copyright © 2021 Prayer M. Madueke

All rights reserved. No part of this work may be reproduced or transmitted in any form or by any means without written permission from the publisher unless otherwise indicated, all Scripture quotations are taken from the King James Version of the Bible, and used by permission. All emphasis within quotations is the author's additions.

ISBN: 979-8513528951

Published by **Prayer Publications**

259 Wainwright Street, Newark,

New Jersey 07112 United States.

MESSAGE FROM THE AUTHOR

PRAYER M. MADUEKE
CHRISTIAN AUTHOR

My name is Prayer Madueke, a spiritual warrior in the Lord's vineyard, an accomplished author, speaker, and expert on spiritual warfare and deliverance. I have published well over 100 books on every area of successful Christian living. I am an acclaimed family and relationship counselor with several titles dealing with critical areas in the lives of the children of God. I travel to several countries each year speaking and conducting deliverance sessions, breaking the yokes of demonic oppression and setting captives free.

It would be a delight to collaborate with you or your ministry in organized crusades, ceremonies, marriages and marriage seminars, special events, church ministration and fellowship for the advancement of God's kingdom here on earth.

You can find all my books on Amazon.com. Feel free to visit my website www.madueke.com for devotionals and other materials.

They have produced many testimonies and I want your testimony to be one too. God bless you.

PRAYER REQUESTS OR COUNSELLING

Send me an email on prayermadu@yahoo.com if you need prayers or counselling or you have any questions.

TABLE OF CONTENTS

1. The Reality of Satanic Courts 1
2. Believers are Destined to Overthrow the Devil 5
3. Decree & Declarations 20

ONE

THE REALITY OF SATANIC COURTS

All believers who truly repent and follow Christ are empowered and appointed to dethrone the devil, and his verdicts in the heavenly courts. The heavenly courts here are not in the heaven where God lives but in the atmospheric heaven. This is the second heaven where the devil and his fallen angels live. This is the heaven where principalities, rulers of the darkness of this world, and powers in charge of spiritual wickedness in the high places emanate from. It is where the prince of the kingdom of Persia withstood God's angelic messenger in the time of Daniel when he prayed for twenty-one days.

> "Then said he unto me, Fear not, Daniel: for from the first day that thou didst set thine heart to understand, and to chasten thyself before thy God, thy words were heard, and I am come for thy words. But the prince of the kingdom of Persia withstood me one and twenty days: but, lo, Michael, one of the chief princes, came to help me; and I remained there with the kings of Persia"
>
> — DANIEL 10:12-13

> "Now is the judgment of this world: now shall the prince of this world be cast out. Hereafter I will not talk much with you: for the prince of this world cometh, and hath nothing in me."
>
> — JOHN 12:31; 14:30

Satan, through an organized network, always judges people in his different courts in the heavenly places to deny them of God's plan, purpose and rights erecting evil roadblocks in the heavenly places. Believers are empowered to enter into the battlefield like Daniel did to confront and conquer Satan's evil utterances in the heavenly courts of the satanic kingdom.

Whatever is said on earthly evil altars, whatever enchantments, divinations and conclusions must be challenged before believers can live in victory over the devil here on earth. As a believer in Christ, you are being followed and monitored by Christ to confirm his words.

> "After these things the Lord appointed (to the) other seventy also, and sent them two and two before his face into every city and place, whither he himself would come. And the seventy returned again with joy, saying, Lord, even the devils are subject unto us through thy name. And he said unto them, I beheld Satan as lightning fall from heaven. Behold, I give unto you power to tread on serpents and scorpions, and over all the power of the enemy: and nothing shall by any means hurt you."
>
> — LUKE 10:1, 17-19;

> "And these signs shall follow them that believe; In my name shall they cast out devils; they shall speak with new tongues; They shall take up serpents; and if they drink any deadly thing, it shall not hurt them; they shall lay hands on the

> sick, and they shall recover. So then after the Lord had spoken unto them, he was received up into heaven, and sat on the right hand of God. And they went forth, and preached everywhere, the Lord working with them, and confirming the word with signs following. Amen."
>
> — MARK 16:17-20

Believers have power to heal the sick, deliver the oppressed and bring God's kingdom down here on earth. The first seventy disciples of Christ exercised this power and had testimonies. The devil obeyed their commands and submitted to their authority through the name of Christ. Christ has given this power to every generation of believers. They can expel demons, tread on serpents and scorpions and overcome the power of the enemy and not get hurt by them. Everywhere you go as a believer, signs will follow you and you can cast out demons in the name of Jesus.

TWO

BELIEVERS ARE DESTINED TO OVERTHROW THE DEVIL

God, in the beginning, gave man dominion over the devil, the devil's agents, and over all creatures. This foundational dominion was interrupted when Adam broke the first commandment by eating the forbidden fruit in the garden of Eden.

> "And God blessed them, and God said unto them, be fruitful, and multiply, and replenish the earth, and subdue it: and have dominion over the fish of the sea, and over the fowl of the air, and over every living thing that moveth upon the earth. Now the serpent was more subtil than

any beast of the field which the Lord God had made. And he said unto the woman, Yea, hath God said, Ye shall not eat of every tree of the garden? And the woman said unto the serpent, we may eat of the fruit of the trees of the garden: But of the fruit of the tree which is in the midst of the garden, God hath said, Ye shall not eat of it, neither shall ye touch it, lest ye die. And the serpent said unto the woman, Ye shall not surely die: For God doth know that in the day ye eat thereof, then your eyes shall be opened, and ye shall be as gods, knowing good and evil. And when the woman saw that the tree was good for food, and that it was pleasant to the eyes, and a tree to be desired to make one wise, she took of the fruit thereof, and did eat, and gave also unto her husband with her; and he did eat. And the eyes of them both were opened, and they knew that they were naked; and they sewed fig leaves together, and made themselves aprons. And they heard the voice of the Lord God walking in the garden in the cool of the day: and Adam and his wife hid themselves from the presence of the Lord God amongst the trees of the garden."

— GENESIS 1:28; 3:1-6

However, Jesus came and restored this lost dominion to mankind. This is available to believers when they repent, forsake their sins and embrace Christ. Without fully understanding what a believer's dominion entails and how to reign over all creatures, you will be kept in bondage. All believers have this right to dominion but may lack the fitness to dominate due to ignorance.

> "My people are destroyed for lack of knowledge: because thou hast rejected knowledge, I will also reject thee, that thou shalt be no priest to me: seeing thou hast forgotten the law of thy God, I will also forget thy children."
>
> — HOSEA 4:6

Many believers do not know the right action required and the way to exercise total dominion over the devil. As a believer, you must first know and believe that it is possible to have dominion over the devil and all his work.

> "That the God of our Lord Jesus Christ, the Father of glory, may give unto you the spirit of wisdom and revelation in the knowledge of him: The eyes of your understanding being enlightened; that ye may know what is the hope of his calling, and what the riches of the glory of his inheritance in the saints, And what is the exceeding greatness of his power to us-ward who believe, according to the working of his mighty power, Which he wrought in Christ, when he raised him from the dead, and set him at his own right hand in the heavenly places, Far above all principality, and power, and might, and dominion, and every name that is named, not only in this world, but also in that which is to come: And hath put all things under his feet, and gave him to be the head over all things to the church, Which is his body, the fulness of him that filleth all in all."
>
> — EPHESIANS 1:17-23

When you lack the true knowledge of God and his son Jesus Christ, your ability to have dominion over the devil will be hindered. This makes you vulnerable to satanic powers and evil activities here on earth. When you accept the call as a believer, you inherit the nature of Christ. This gives you dominion over the devil. If you know your position in Christ as a son of God, brother to Jesus, the beloved of God, a King, an ambassador and an heir to God, you will stop underestimating yourself before the devil.

> "Now therefore ye are no more strangers and foreigners, but fellow citizens with the saints, and of the household of God."
>
> — EPHESIANS 2:19

To overthrow the devil and live in dominion over his evil activities, you must first of all deal with your sinful nature. You must understand that sin is first inherited before it is committed. You must believe that sin can be dealt with from the foundation, and can be conquered by the power that is in the blood of Jesus.

> "Now the works of the flesh are manifest, which are these; Adultery, fornication, uncleanness, lasciviousness, Idolatry, witchcraft, hatred, variance, emulations, wrath, strife, seditions,

> heresies, Envyings, murders, drunkenness, revellings, and such like: of the which I tell you before, as I have also told you in time past, that they which do such things shall not inherit the kingdom of God."
>
> — GALATIANS 5:19-21

The works of the flesh are mentioned here because Christ wants us to overcome them and be free of their influence while we are on earth. While sinners are called to repentance, repentant believers who are already in Christ are called to overcome the works of the flesh and live holy on earth.

> "For God hath not called us unto uncleanness, but unto holiness. He therefore that despiseth, despiseth not man, but God, who hath also given unto us his holy Spirit."
>
> — 1 THESSALONIANS 4:7-8

If God has not given you power to overcome the works of the flesh which are enemies of holiness, He would not call you unto holiness. One of the things that hinders your holiness as a believer is the unbelief that you can be holy. Because of the unbelief, many believers despise the doctrine of holiness and deny themselves God's provision for living holy. To overthrow the devil, you must have dominion over sin. Unfortunately, many forget this important condition and seek only physical dominion. Believers can have dominion over the powers of the devil and prosper physically but some sins will still have dominion over them. True deliverance and victory over the devil are rooted in dominion over the works of the flesh.

> "We know that whosoever is born of God sinneth not; but he that is begotten of God keepeth himself, and that wicked one toucheth him not."
>
> — 1 JOHN 5:18

> "What shall we say then? Shall we continue in sin, that grace may abound? God forbids. How shall we, that are dead to sin, live any longer therein? Know ye not, that so many of us as were baptized into Jesus Christ were baptized into his death? Therefore, we are buried with him by baptism into death: that like as Christ was raised up from the dead by the glory of the

> Father, even so we also should walk in newness of life. Likewise reckon ye also yourselves to be dead indeed unto sin, but alive unto God through Jesus Christ our Lord."
>
> — ROMANS 6:1-4, 11

The popular saying by some believers that we are like a fish in the water, with flesh and blood and cannot stop committing sin, is not from God but from the devil. You are forbidden from committing sin as soon as you become born again.

Does it mean that a sanctified and born-again child of God cannot backslide and fall into sin? A child of God can fall into sin but there is a provision to bounce back and continue with God, without giving the devil a place in one's life.

> "And Paul, earnestly beholding the council, said, Men and brethren, I have lived in all good conscience before God until this day. And the high priest Ananias commanded them that stood by him to smite him on the mouth. Then said Paul unto him, God shall smite thee, thou whited wall: for sittest thou to judge me after the law, and commandest me to be smitten

contrary to the law? And they that stood by said, Revilest thou God's high priest? Then said Paul, I wist not, brethren, that he was the high priest: for it is written, thou shalt not speak evil of the ruler of thy people."

— ACTS 23:1-5

"My little children, these things write I unto you, that ye sin not. And if any man sin, we have an advocate with the Father, Jesus Christ the righteous: And he is the propitiation for our sins: and not for ours only, but also for the sins of the whole world."

— 1 JOHN 2:1-2

When the high priest Ananias commanded that Paul should be smitten in the mouth, which is wrong, Paul's old nature manifested and he used his tongue wrongly. But when he realized he was wrong, he did not argue, look for excuses or shift blame. Instead, he quickly accepted his mistake and apologized. Though a seasoned lawyer, he never focused on the fault of the high priest and even if he must, his own error must be accepted and quickly dealt with. This was done and right away; he was convicted of the sin of speaking wrongly against the high priest. As a result, the devil who is the accuser of the brethren couldn't approach God for permission to attack Paul, because Paul's sin was not recorded against him. He had confessed it. The confession of a believer's sins may take a short or long time, but once they are confessed, they manifest the fruit of the Spirit, not the flesh.

> "But the fruit of the Spirit is love, joy, peace, longsuffering, gentleness, goodness, faith, Meekness, temperance: against such there is no law.
>
> — GALATIANS." 5:22-23

When you confront unbelievers with their sins, what they have will manifest, which are the works of the flesh. At that point, the devil will approach God for permission to attack them with all kinds of problems. At times, the devil may not attack them immediately but prosper them with fake blessings. Their suffering and punishment come when they least expect them. The sins of believers are not counted or held against them because of their humility and manifestation of God's Spirit. The Lord Jesus Christ is the advocate of every believer. This is why sins and errors are never recorded against believers by the devil.

> "He that committeth sin is of the devil; for the devil sinneth from the beginning. For this purpose, the Son of God was manifested, that he might destroy the works of the devil. Whosoever is born of God doth not commit sin; for his seed remaineth in him: and he cannot sin, because he is born of God."
>
> — 1 JOHN 3:8-9

Believers deal with sin once and for all and cannot continue in sin like sinners who are under bondage of sin. The seed of God is always in a believer. A believer is not a sinner or just one who goes to church without knowing what it is all about. A believer is a citizen of heaven with heavenly character. He is directed by the Spirit of God. A believer is converted and separated from evil activities in the world. He is born again. His heart is regenerated and transformed. True believers walk daily in the light of the word of God. He has no desire any longer to live for self but rather lives for God. He has his heart fixed on the things of the kingdom. Believers hate sin, love the word of God, and avoid sin like a plague. Sinners love sin and are dominated by the power of sin. Believers are led by the Holy Spirit. Sinners do not have a sense of spiritual value. They lack self-control and live like animals.

> "Mortify therefore your members which are upon the earth; fornication, uncleanness, inordinate affection, evil concupiscence, and covetousness, which is idolatry: For which things' sake the wrath of God cometh on the children of disobedience: In the which ye also walked some time, when ye lived in them. But now ye also put off all these; anger, wrath, malice, blasphemy, filthy communication out of your mouth. Lie not one to another, seeing that ye have put off the old man with his deeds; And have put on the new man, which is renewed in knowledge after the image of him that created him."
>
> — COLOSSIANS 3:5-10

Sinners commit sin with joy, without feeling guilty but true believers avoid sin, feel guilty and condemned when overcome by sin. They do everything possible to return to righteousness (Psalms 51:1-19). Sinners are soaked in the things of the world. They lust after the flesh. The eyes do all kinds of evil without feeling guilty. Sinners are covetous, proud of their positions, power, self-righteous, and greedy for riches.

True believers are gentle, tender, kind, cultured, refined in character, and compassionate. They apply self-control in the indulgence of appetites and passions. They hate the evils of the world system. The world we talk about here is not the created universe, not the sum total of human beings who inhabit the earth, but the society organized without reference to God.

> "These things I have spoken unto you, that in me ye might have peace. In the world ye shall have tribulation: but be of good cheer; I have overcome the world."
>
> — JOHN 16:33

To overcome the world means to refuse partake in evil activities on earth. It is refusal to compromise God's standards. After overcoming sin, your prayers to overthrow Satan, sickness, diseases and the works of the devil and his agents will be speedily answered

> "And the seventy returned again with joy, saying, Lord, even the devils are subject unto us through thy name. And he said unto them, I beheld Satan as lightning fall from heaven. Behold, I give unto you power to tread on serpents and scorpions, and over all the power of the enemy: and nothing shall by any means hurt you."
>
> — LUKE 10:17-19

> "And God blessed them, and God said unto them, be fruitful, and multiply, and replenish the earth, and subdue it: and have dominion over the fish of the sea, and over the fowl of the air, and over every living thing that moveth upon the earth."
>
> — GENESIS 1:28

When God created man, his purpose was for man to have dominion over the devil on earth. This dominion was lost by Adam but Christ died to restore it. Therefore, Christian life started with dominion and total victory over the devil. This dominion must be exercised diligently and consistently by true believers who know their right and position here on earth.

THREE

DECREE & DECLARATIONS

Every satanic roadblock against my destiny in heaven, or under heaven, be dismantled by force, in the name of Jesus. Any evil movement anywhere among creation, be demobilized immediately. Every satanic material before me, catch fire and burn to ashes, in the mighty name of Jesus. Father Lord, release your heavenly soldiers to fight for me in the atmospheric heaven and here on earth. Ability to pray, fast and engage in all manner of prayers to destroy the last enemies in the battlefield of my life, possess me, in the name of Jesus.

> "In the third year of Cyrus king of Persia a thing was revealed unto Daniel, whose name was called Belteshazzar; and the thing was true, but

the time appointed was long: and he understood the thing, and had understanding of the vision. In those days, I, Daniel was mourning three full weeks. I ate no pleasant bread, neither came flesh nor wine in my mouth, neither did I anoint myself at all, till three whole weeks were fulfilled."

— DANIEL 10:1-3

"When Mordecai perceived all that was done, Mordecai rent his clothes, and put on sackcloth with ashes, and went out into the midst of the city, and cried with a loud and a bitter cry; And came even before the king's gate: for none might enter into the king's gate clothed with sackcloth. And in every province, whithersoever the king's commandment and his decree came, there was great mourning among the Jews, and fasting, and weeping, and wailing; and many lay in sackcloth and ashes. Then Mordecai commanded to answer Esther, think not with thyself that thou shalt escape in the king's house, more than all the Jews. For if thou altogether holdest thy peace at this time, then shall there enlargement and deliverance arise to

> the Jews from another place; but thou and thy father's house shall be destroyed: and who knoweth whether thou art come to the kingdom for such a time as this? Then Esther bade them return Mordecai this answer, Go, gather together all the Jews that are present in Shushan, and fast ye for me, and neither eat nor drink three days, night or day: I also and my maidens will fast likewise; and so will I go in unto the king, which is not according to the law: and if I perish, I perish. So, Mordecai went his way, and did according to all that Esther had commanded him."

— ESTHER 4:1-3, 13-17

Father Lord, open my eyes to see my enemy's stronghold and empower me to destroy them, in the name of Jesus. I receive the best understanding to handle every situation keeping me in bondage. Every organized darkness that has vowed to block my blessings anywhere in creation, be disorganized. Any spiritual and physical mountain standing before me, be demolished by the power of God, in the name of Jesus. Any mysterious weakness in my life to keep me out of divine action against the powers of darkness, be destroyed. I break and loose myself from any power holding me down from taking action against my stubborn enemy, in the name of Jesus.

> "And I say also unto thee, that thou art Peter, and upon this rock I will build my church; and the gates of hell shall not prevail against it. And I will give unto thee the keys of the kingdom of heaven: and whatsoever thou shalt bind on earth shall be bound in heaven: and whatsoever thou shalt loose on earth shall be loosed in heaven."
>
> — MATTHEW 16:18-19

Any evil gate, doors and windows installed by the devil and his agents to block my way to prosperity, be destroyed by fire, in the name of Jesus. Almighty God, burn to ashes every gate of hell blocking me from reaching my goals in life. Every demon standing against me, your time is up, I bind and cast you, in the name of Jesus. Lord arise and take me to my place in life, by your power. Let the backbone of spiritual forces against me be broken to pieces. I break and release myself from any evil power holding me down from acting against their evil against me, in the name of Jesus.

Ancient of days, by your mercy, send me an angelic assistant to help me on the battlefield, in the name of Jesus. By your mercy O Lord, appear on the battlefield of my life to terminate the activities of the devil and his agents. Let the evil forces against me be frustrated by the anointing of the Holy Ghost, in the name of Jesus.

> "And in the four and twentieth day of the first month, as I was by the side of the great river, which is Hiddekel; Then I lifted up mine eyes, and looked, and behold a certain man clothed in linen, whose loins were girded with fine gold of Uphaz: His body also was like the beryl, and his face as the appearance of lightning, and his eyes as lamps of fire, and his arms and his feet like in color to polished brass, and the voice of his words like the voice of a multitude."
>
> — DANIEL 10:4-6

Almighty God, help me to be rightly engaged at the right place and at the right time, in the name of Jesus. I command the angel of war, trained to kill to come down and help me in the battles of life. Every satanic deposit preventing me from warring against the devil, catch fire, burn to ashes, and release me now, in the name of Jesus. Every good thing I have lost in the battle of life, I recover you double. Father Lord, show yourself in my case and save me from merciless and determined enemies, in the name of Jesus. Let the voice of victory from heaven manifest on the battlefield of my life and deliver me from every problem that is stronger than me. Almighty God, roar from the third heaven against the judgment passed against me from satanic altars, in the name of Jesus.

> "And I turned to see the voice that spake with me. And being turned, I saw seven golden candlesticks; And in the midst of the seven candlesticks one like unto the Son of man, clothed with a garment down to the foot, and girt about the paps with a golden girdle. His head and his hairs were white like wool, as white as snow; and his eyes were as a flame of fire; And his feet like unto fine brass, as if they burned in a furnace; and his voice as the sound of many waters."
>
> — REVELATION 1:12-15

Let the voice of destruction visit satanic soldiers that have risen against my destiny in the name of Jesus. Lord Jesus, by your mercy, speak from the third heaven against every negative utterance ever spoken against me. Every satanic weapon prepared against me by the devil and his agents, catch fire and burn to ashes now. By the mercy of the Almighty God, let the sound of victory from heaven destroy evil voices against me from the camp of my enemies, in the name of Jesus. Let the voice of God by his mercy, overthrow every demonic voice speaking against my existence in Jesus name.

Father Lord, let your presence in my life destroy every evil presence assigned to frustrate my destiny, in the name of Jesus. Let the power of God appear on the battlefield of my life and overpower every stubborn enemy with the determination to waste my life. Ancient of days, release your whirlwind to blow away every evil presence organized against my destiny, in the mighty name of Jesus.

> "And I Daniel alone saw the vision: for the men that were with me saw not the vision; but a great quaking fell upon them, so that they fled to hide themselves. Therefore, I was left alone, and saw this great vision, and there remained no strength in me: for my comeliness was

turned in me into corruption, and I retained no strength. Yet heard I the voice of his words: and when I heard the voice of his words, then was I in a deep sleep on my face, and my face toward the ground."

— DANIEL 10:7-9

"And as he journeyed, he came near Damascus: and suddenly there shined round about him a light from heaven: And he fell to the earth, and heard a voice saying unto him, Saul, Saul, why persecutest thou me? And he said, Who art thou, Lord? And the Lord said, I am Jesus whom thou persecutest: it is hard for thee to kick against the pricks. And he trembling and astonished said, Lord, what wilt thou have me to do? And the Lord said unto him, Arise, and go into the city, and it shall be told thee what thou must do. And the men which journeyed with him stood speechless, hearing a voice, but seeing no man."

— ACTS 9:3-7

Let divine earthquake from heaven visit the headquarters of the enemy that has vowed to eliminate my life, in the name of Jesus. Any evil program going on against my destiny, be terminated by divine voice immediately. I command every demon on the battlefield of my life to flee and turn back no more, in the name of Jesus. Let all the evil spirit ministering against me from my foundation and place of birth leave now by force without delay. Every good thing that the devil and his agents has denied me over the years, I recover you double, in the name of Jesus. I command the voice and the presence of the devil to cease forever in my life by the voice of God. Every strength I have lost in the battle field of life, I recover you double, in the name of Jesus.

> "As the appearance of the bow that is in the cloud in the day of rain, so was the appearance of the brightness roundabout. This was the appearance of the likeness of the glory of the Lord. And when I saw it, I fell upon my face, and I heard a voice of one that spake. And he said unto me, Son of man, stand upon thy feet, and I will speak unto thee. And the spirit entered into me when he spake unto me, and set me upon my feet, that I heard him that spake unto me. And he said unto me, Son of man, I send thee to

> the children of Israel, to a rebellious nation that hath rebelled against me: they and their fathers have transgressed against me, even unto this very day."
>
> — EZEKIEL 1:28; 2:1-3

Any journey organized by my enemy against my destiny, be terminated in defeat by the mercy of God, in the name of Jesus. Let the light of God for judgment overpower my enemies and turn their darkness unto a shining light. Every evil strength moving my enemies against me, disappear without notice and abandon them with mysterious weakness, in the name of Jesus. I command my enemies to collapse and rise up unto repentance or remain under divine judgment until they repent. Any persecution going on against me anywhere, be terminated unto repentance or unto judgment against my persecutors, in the name of Jesus. I release the rain of sorrow and destruction upon all my unrepentant enemies. Every good thing within and around my determined enemies, what are you waiting for? Disappear, in the name of Jesus. I command all my repentant enemies to swallow the word of God and repent by the power of God, in the name of Jesus.

Messengers from the third heaven, touch me, strengthen me and destroy my weaknesses by your mercy, in the name of Jesus. Almighty God, give me a testimony that will encourage me to fight more and elicit the "How did it happen?" response from people. I command every evil hand stretched towards me to dry up by fire and let the hand of God rest upon me, for the rest of my life, in the name of Jesus. Every enemy of divine program in my life, be exposed and disgraced.

> "And, behold, an hand touched me, which set me upon my knees and upon the palms of my hands. And he said unto me, O Daniel, a man greatly beloved, understand the words that I speak unto thee, and stand upright: for unto thee am I now sent. And when he had spoken this word unto me, I stood trembling."
>
> — DANIEL 10:10-11

Any evil spirit assigned to follow me around, I bind and cast you out in the name of Jesu. Blood of Jesus, speak me out of every satanic limitation, in the mighty name of Jesus. Ancient of days, deliver me from every satanic prison. I break and loose myself from every satanic verdict, in the name of Jesus. You the gods of my father's house, ancestral gods assigned against me, be frustrated, in the name of Jesus. Every satanic judgment prospering in my life, fail woefully. Almighty God, take me away from satanic domain and bring me to a place of freedom, in the name of Jesus. Let the judgment against my life from heavenly places be reversed in my favor, in the name of Jesus-

> "Hereafter I will not talk much with you: for the prince of this world cometh, and hath nothing in me."
>
> — JOHN 14:30

> "In whom the god of this world hath blinded the minds of them which believe not, lest the light of the glorious gospel of Christ, who is the image of God, should shine unto them."
>
> — 2 CORINTHIANS 4:4

> "Wherein in time past ye walked according to the course of this world, according to the prince of the power of the air, the spirit that now worketh in the children of disobedience: For we wrestle not against flesh and blood, but

> against principalities, against powers, against the rulers of the darkness of this world, against spiritual wickedness in high places."
>
> — EPHESIANS 2:2; 6:12

I command all the fallen angels assigned against me to be disgraced forever, in the name of Jesus. You the prince of darkness opposing God's will in my life, I bind and cast you out. Almighty God, send your guardian angel to guide me to my place of rest and victory, in the name of Jesus. Let the rulers of darkness fighting against my settlement and establishment be disappointed. Lord, arise and move my life forward by your mercy. Any part of my life captured by sickness and disease, be released by fire, in the name of Jesus.

Let the organized network of the devil against my life be disorganized unto destruction forever and ever, in the name of Jesus. You the prince of this world on assignment to stop the move of God in my life, I bind and cast you out. Anything in me inviting Satan and problems into my life, catch fire and burn to ashes, in the name of Jesus. Almighty God, empower me to say no against sin and maintain my stand forever. Any evil force fighting against my obedience to God's commandment, I bind and cast you out, in the name of Jesus.

Ancient of Days, deliver me from spiritual blindness and demonic deafness, in the name of Jesus. Let the light of the gospel enlighten my mind and bring freedom to my soul and Spirit. Every enemy against the manifestation of divine light and God's glory in my life, be frustrated, in the name of Jesus. You the prince of the powers of the air causing me to walk contrary to God's will, I bind and cast you out. You the spirit that promotes disobedience against God's plan and divine purpose for my life, I bind and cast you out. I reverse every satanic judgment ever pronounced against me by the devil and his agents, living or dead, in the name of Jesus.

Any evil force, wrestling against God's plans for my life, scatter and perish, in the name of Jesus. I command the judgments of principalities, powers, rulers of darkness of this world and their agents against me to fail woefully, expire and backfire, in the name of Jesus. Father Lord, thank you for your power in my life over the devil. I command the devil and his work to come under me. Blood of Jesus, use me to disgrace the devil anywhere I go. You the devil in any department of my life, be dethroned, in the name of Jesus.

Let the hidden works of the devil in my life be exposed in Jesus name. I deliver my destiny from the control of the devil and his agents. Any evil mark in my life from the devil, clear away now, in the name of Jesus. By the power of God in my life, I dethrone the devil in my life. Any power of the devil ruling over my life, be destroyed. I dethrone every evil throne in my life by fire, in the name of Jesus. Almighty God, deliver me from the reign of the devil forever. Almighty God, use me to dethrone the devil anywhere any time, in the name of Jesus. Let the host of heaven arise and use me to destroy the works of the devil. Father Lord, empower my voice to deliver the captives, in the name of Jesus.

Every determined enemy, wherever you are in my life, bow, in the name of Jesus. Any evil pregnancy in my life, be aborted immediately. Any weapon of darkness secretly destroying me, be exposed and destroyed. Any evil prophesy to bring me under the devil, I reject you. Every demonic invisible wall built around me, collapse, in the name of Jesus. Let all evil spirits mobilized against me be disgraced. Any agent of the devil that has vowed to end my life, end your own life, in the name of Jesus.

Evil powers, sitting upon my place in life, be unseated now, in the name of Jesus. Any spiritual warfare going on against me, be terminated. Any arrow of death fired against my life, return back to your sender. Every demonic dominion over my life, end immediately, in the name of Jesus. You my deliverance under evil control, escape now. Every demonic pronouncement over my life, be terminated. Let all demonic positioning against me be repositioned in my favor, in the name of Jesus.

Every good thing stolen from me by the devil, I recover you now in Jesus name. Every satanic investment in my life, receive destruction now, in the name of Jesus.

THANK YOU!

I'd like to use this time to thank you for purchasing my books and helping my ministry and work. Any copy of my book you buy helps to fund my ministry and family, as well as offering much-needed inspiration to keep writing. My family and I are very thankful, and we take your assistance very seriously.

Thank you so much as you spare this precious moment of your time and may God bless you and meet you at every point of your need.

Send me an email on prayermadu@yahoo.com if you need prayers or counsel or you have questions. Better still if you want to be friends with me.

OTHER BOOKS BY PRAYER MADUEKE

1. 100 Days Prayers to Wake Up Your Lazarus
2. 15 Deliverance Steps to Everlasting Life
3. 21/40 Nights of Decrees and Your Enemies Will Surrender
4. 35 Deliverance Steps to Everlasting Rest
5. 35 Special Dangerous Decrees
6. 40 Prayer Giants
7. Alone with God
8. Americans, May I Have Your Attention Please
9. Avoid Academic Defeats
10. Because You Are Living Abroad
11. Biafra of My Dream
12. Breaking Evil Yokes
13. Call to Renew Covenant
14. Command the Morning, Day and Night
15. Community Liberation and Solemn Assembly
16. Comprehensive Deliverance
17. Confront and Conquer Your Enemy
18. Contemporary Politicians' Prayers for Nation Building
19. Crossing the Hurdles
20. Dangerous Decrees to Destroy Your Destroyers (Series)
21. Dealing with Institutional Altars
22. Deliverance by Alpha and Omega

23. Deliverance from Academic Defeats
24. Deliverance from Compromise
25. Deliverance from Luke warmness
26. Deliverance from The Devil and His Agents
27. Deliverance from The Spirit of Jezebel
28. Deliverance Letters 1
29. Deliverance Letters 2
30. Deliverance Through Warning in Advance
31. Evil Summon
32. Foundation Exposed (Part 1)
33. Foundations Exposed (Part 2)
34. Healing Covenant
35. International Women's Prayer Network
36. Leviathan The Beast
37. Ministers Empowerment Prayer Network
38. More Kingdoms to Conquer
39. Organized Student in a Disorganized School
40. Pray for a New Nigeria
41. Pray for Jamaica
42. Pray for Trump, America, Israel and Yourself
43. Pray for Your Country
44. Pray for Your Pastor and Yourself
45. Prayer Campaign for a Better Ghana
46. Prayer Campaign for a Better Kenya
47. Prayer Campaign for Nigeria
48. Prayer Campaign for Uganda

49. Prayer Retreat
50. Prayers Against Premature Death
51. Prayers Against Satanic Oppression
52. Prayers for a Happy Married Life
53. Prayers for a Job Interview
54. Prayers for a Successful Career
55. Prayers for Academic Success
56. Prayers for an Excellent Job
57. Prayers for Breakthrough in Your Business
58. Prayers for Children and Youths
59. Prayers for Christmas
60. Prayers for College and University Students
61. Prayers for Conception and Power to Retain
62. Prayers for Deliverance
63. Prayers for Fertility in Your Marriage
64. Prayers for Financial Breakthrough
65. Prayers for Good Health
66. Prayers for Marriage and Family
67. Prayers for Marriages in Distress
68. Prayers for Mercy
69. Prayers for Nation Building
70. Prayers for Newly Married Couple
71. Prayers for Overcoming Attitude Problem
72. Prayers for Political Excellence and Veteran Politicians (Prayers for Nation Building Book 2)
73. Prayers for Pregnant Women

74. Prayers for Restoration of Peace in Marriage
75. Prayers for Sound Sleep and Rest
76. Prayers for Success in Examination
77. Prayers for Widows and Orphans
78. Prayers for Your Children's Deliverance
79. Prayers to Buy a Home and Settle Down
80. Prayers to Conceive and Bear Children
81. Prayers to Deliver Your Child Safely
82. Prayers to End a Prolonged Pregnancy
83. Prayers to Enjoy Your Wealth and Riches
84. Prayers to Experience Love in Your Marriage
85. Prayers to Get Married Happily
86. Prayers to Heal Broken Relationship
87. Prayers to Keep Your Marriage Out of Trouble
88. Prayers to Live an Excellent Life
89. Prayers to Live and End Your Life Well
90. Prayers to Marry Without Delay
91. Prayers to Overcome an Evil Habit
92. Prayers to Overcome Attitude Problems
93. Prayers to Overcome Miscarriage
94. Prayers to Pray During Honeymoon
95. Prayers to Preserve Your Marriage
96. Prayers to Prevent Separation of Couples
97. Prayers to Progress in Your Career
98. Prayers to Raise Godly Children
99. Prayers to Receive Financial Miracle

100. Prayers to Retain Your Pregnancy
101. Prayers to Triumph Over Divorce
102. Queen of Heaven: Wife of Satan
103. School for Children Teachers
104. School for Church Workers
105. School for Women of Purpose: Women
106. School for Youths and Students
107. School of Deliverance with Eternity in View
108. School of Ministry for Ministers in Ministry
109. School of Prayer
110. Speaking Things into Existence (Series)
111. Special Prayers in His Presence
112. Tears in Prison: Prisoners of Hope
113. The First Deliverance
114. The Operation of the Woman That Sit Upon Many Waters
115. The Philosophy of Deliverance
116. The Reality of Spirit Marriage
117. The Sword of New Testament Deliverance
118. Two Prosperities
119. Upon All These Prayers
120. Veteran Politicians' Prayers for Nation Building
121. Welcome to Campus
122. When Evil Altars Are Multiplied
123. When I Grow Up Visions
124. You Are a Man's Wife

125. Your Dream Directory
126. Youths, May I Have Your Attention Please?

AN INVITATION TO BECOME A MINISTRY PARTNER

In response to several calls from readers of my books on how to collaborate with this ministry, we are grateful to provide our ministry's bank details.

Be assured that our continued prayers for you will be answered according to God's Word, and as you remain faithful by sowing seeds of faith, God will never forget your labors of love in Christ Jesus.

Send your Seeds to:

In Nigeria & Africa

Bank Name: **Access Bank**

Account Name: **Prayer Emancipation Missions**

Account Number: **0692638220**

In the United States & the rest of the World

Bank Name: **Bank of America**

Account Name: **Roseline C. Madueke**

Account Number: **483079070578**

You can also visit the donation page on my website to donate online: www.madueke.com/donate.

Made in the USA
Columbia, SC
11 August 2021